SWANSEA CITY
Road to Wembley

SWANSEA CITY
Road to Wembley

HUW BOWEN

Gomer

Published in 2013 by
Gomer Press, Llandysul, Ceredigion, SA44 4JL

ISBN: 978 1 84851 735 6

A CIP record for this title is available from the British Library.
© Copyright text: Huw Bowen 2013

Huw Bowen asserts his moral right under the
Copyright, Designs and Patents Act, 1988
to be identified as author of this work.

The John Hartson Foundation is a company limited by
guarantee and having charitable status. Registered charity in
England and Wales. Charity No: 1151319. Website: www.
johnhartsonfoundation.co.uk.

This book is published with the financial support of the
Welsh Books Council.

Printed and bound in Wales at
Gomer Press, Llandysul, Ceredigion

This book is dedicated to the
North Bank and all those Jacks who stood there
between 1912 and 2005.

Acknowledgements

First of all, I would like to thank the players, directors and backroom staff of Swansea City for making a great number of people happy beyond their wildest dreams. What has been achieved by the Swans over the last ten years or so is nothing short of miraculous, and, as a long-suffering fan, I am truly grateful. I owe a great debt to Alan Edmunds and Ceri Gould of the *Western Mail*/MediaWales for allowing me to fill their newspaper with my Swans-related ramblings over six days in the run-up to the Wembley final. As ever, it has been a pleasure working with them.

It has also been a pleasure working with my colleague and long-distance cycling companion Huw Morris, who took the lead in organising the great Jackademics expedition to Wembley. Since then we have set up YJB Travel, Tours, and Exports, and I look forward to our forthcoming foray(s) into Europe. I thank Jon Price of Dorian Heel Bar, Oxford Street, Swansea, whose range of Swans T-shirts and memorabilia is truly stupendous. I owe a special culinary debt to Cathy Long and Steve Morris, who supplied the excellent pasties at Wembley. As ever, Huw Cooze of Visions Creative and the Swans Supporters Trust has been immensely helpful and supportive, as has Tony Woolway, the picture librarian at the *Western Mail*, despite the fact that his footballing loyalties quite obviously lie with those who cannot be mentioned. I am very grateful to Colin Jones for granting me access to his magnificent Swans photograph collection, and to Phil Bethell and Martin Johnes of the Swans 100 Centenary Project for providing me with images of programme covers. All photographs or images are copyright *Western Mail*/Media Wales except as noted: Swans 100 project: pages 17, 23, 28, 45, 52; Mike Floate: page 30; Huw Bowen: pages 46, 50, 60; Elizabeth Stead: page 54; Dave Roberts: page 61; Huw Morris: pages 65, 71; Martin Johnes: page 66; Peter Charles: pages 67, 68, 69; Helen Baldwin: page 70; Huw Jones, pages 76-77.

At Gwasg Gomer, I wish to thank Jonathan Lewis and Ceri Wyn Jones for their enthusiastic support for this enterprise, and I am especially indebted to Luned Whelan, a Swans fan who at very short notice pulled things together with great speed and efficiency. Diolch yn fawr iawn.

I thank my long-suffering wife and family for putting up with my Swans obsessive-compulsive behaviour over the last five decades, especially my sister 'Stan', aka Siân Roberts, who cheerfully [*are you sure? Ed.*] allowed me to name and shame her as a 'plastic' in a national newspaper. Above all, I thank the Jackademics who have amused and entertained me before, during and after countless games over many years. They are a complete and utter pain in the arse when it comes to organisation, logistics, and actually handing over the money they owe me, and some of them should be banned from ever owning a mobile phone, but when it comes down to it I luvs 'em all. At this point I should of course stress that the views and opinions expressed in this book are mine and mine alone. They cannot be attributed in any way, shape, or form to anyone else, and most especially, they cannot be attributed to Swansea University.

All royalty payments from the sale of this book will be donated to the John Hartson Foundation. Not only is John Hartson a Jack through and through but since his very public struggle with cancer he has been an inspiration to us all. Big John is a very big man with an even bigger heart. It is just a pity that he never actually played for the Swans. Never mind. Nobody's perfect!

Huw Bowen,
Cloud Nine,
May 2013

Huw Bowen has supported the Swans for forty-five years, although by rights he should have been playing for them. In his spare time, he is Professor of Modern History at Swansea University.

Contents

An Introduction to the John Hartson Foundation   10

From the cradle to the grave:
    the autobiography of a Swans fan   13

Clouds of darkness, clouds of despair:
    keeping a weather eye on Swansea City   20

From the Vetch to the Liberty: a home from home?   28

Heroes: close encounters of the Swans kind   32

The eight most important games in the history of the Swans   46

The diary: Road to Wembley   49

The Capital One Cup final match report   79

Cardiff go up: a view from Swansea   85

The John Hartson Foundation

The Foundation was set up in February 2010 by John following his battle with testicular cancer, which spread to his brain and lungs and left him fighting for life.

John Hartson with the Capital One Cup. What a shame he didn't have a Swans shirt on

During his illness and recovery John and his wife Sarah had first-hand experience of the devastating physical, emotional and financial effects of cancer on those diagnosed with the illness, and their families.

Reports of John's illness and recovery were carried in many national newspapers and he continues to have a prominent public profile. As a well-known sportsman, he decided to use his status as someone who has beaten this devastating illness to provide support and inspiration to others going through the same experience, and to raise money to help people with cancer and their families.

The aim of the Foundation is to raise awareness of the signs and symptoms of testicular cancer in the hope that men with any concerns about their health will see a doctor sooner rather than later, leading to early diagnosis and treatment. It is doing this with a distinctive new logo and call to action – Grab Life by the Balls.

The charity also raises funds to help support people with cancer and their families. One of the first organisations to benefit was the new £3m Maggie's Centre at Swansea's Singleton Hospital, one of a network of Maggie's Centres which provides free practical, emotional and social support for people with cancer and their loved ones.

With its roots in John's native Wales, but a reach that spans the length and breadth of the UK, the Foundation is now managed by a board of trustees including Sarah, while John is busy doing everything he can to draw attention to the charity's work.

I hope that in a small way this book will help to draw attention to the great work being done by John and the Foundation.

FROM THE CRADLE TO THE GRAVE:
THE AUTOBIOGRAPHY OF A SWANS FAN

I am now a fifty-three-year-old bald bloke with glasses, but once upon a time I was going to be the next big thing on the conveyor belt of Swansea soccer talent that had produced the Allchurch brothers, the Charles brothers, Terry Medwin, Cliff Jones, Mel Nurse, Leighton James, Robbie James, and so many others. Unfortunately, however, in school I was forced to play rugby (very badly) and therefore my footballing skills had to be honed in endless one-on-one games against my mate Nick Wroe. These games were played out for hours on end in the car park of the Beaufort Arms in Kittle. Here, I combined the trickery of Brian Evans with the shooting skills of Geoff Thomas and the heading ability of Herbie Williams, and, just for good measure, I became a goalkeeper as agile and athletic as Tony Millington. On the basis of my four-year unbeaten run against the leaden-footed Wroe, which brought me three league championship winners medals, a European cup winners medal, and forty-seven Welsh caps, I assumed that it would be only a matter of time before I was spotted by a passing scout, who would then arrange for me to sign for the Swans or, failing that, Spurs, who were my 'big team'. I would then inspire the Swans to such an extent that they would rise triumphantly from the Fourth Division to the First. This did

Jeremy Charles: it should have been me

13

The class of 1978-79: a great team with a great away kit, as worn here by Tosh, Terry Medwin and Les Chappell

indeed happen, but unfortunately it happened to Jeremy Charles and not to me.

So, instead of actually playing for the Swans as I should have done, I put all my energies into supporting them in the way that we all did in the 1960s and 1970s. I read every word in *Shoot!* magazine and the *Evening Post*, sorry, I meant *Western Mail*. I collected programmes and tickets, I made scrapbooks, and when it was too dark to kick a ball about outside I hammered the hapless Wroe in full-scale Subbuteo competitions that lasted for weeks and took us from the preliminary rounds of the FA Cup to the final. Miraculously, but perhaps not entirely surprisingly, the Swans always seemed to win. And, of course, I went to the Vetch, and not just to the all-important league games but also to friendlies and even to watch the reserves in the league competition known as the Football Combination. I have always wondered about that: combination of what? I suspect that Colin Jones will know the answer.

I have to confess that there were times when my interest wavered, partly because the team was terrible in the mid-1970s, and partly because there were other teenage things to do. But the Swans provided a focus, a structure, and a rhythm to life, and when things picked up again on the pitch in 1976-77 I rarely missed a home game.

Looking back, in many ways the years between 1976 and 1979 provided the best of times. The fast-evolving team seemed to score goals for fun. There were some really good players in addition to the core provided by Curt, Robbie, and Charlo. Two of my favourites were the wingers Kevin Moore and Mickey Conway, although the latter was badly injured in a car accident.

Best of all, the North Bank was always packed and it was always rocking, never more so than during my favourite game of all time, a midweek 4-4 draw against Rotherham. In that epic game, former Swan Dai Gwyther scored a first-half hat-trick for the opposition and the Swans recovered from 4-1 down, with Curt scoring the equaliser just before the end. As if that wasn't enough, four days later the top-of-the-table Swans beat Tranmere 4-3 at the Vetch, having been 3-2 down at half-time. Curt scored the winner in the last few minutes. Happy days.

But things became a bit more complicated when I went to university in Aberystwyth. At first, things were not too difficult because, with the Swans on a seemingly never-ending up under Toshack, travelling to games remained a pleasure, a no-brainer. But when the bubble burst in 1982 and the team plummeted down the leagues, all logic suggested that this was the time to dump the Swans and find something else to do.

The fact that this did not happen is in large part down to one man, my good mate and then neighbour, Mark Thomas. Mark is a Yorkshireman from Doncaster, a Graeme Souness-Lionel Richie-Kevin The Scouser look-a-like, who by all accounts (his own) was once a decent footballer and had played at a good semi-pro level. When I first met him in 1981 he was not only a mainstay of Tregaron Turfs FC but had become an expert gardener and chef, which meant that his wife Diane had very little to do other than file her nails.

Mark is probably the most enthusiastic, positive, and optimistic human being I have ever met, and his support for Donny knows no bounds. In fact, he cannot go more than three sentences without mentioning the word 'Donny' and every five sentences he manages to work in a reference to Alick Jeffrey, his hero and Donny's great goal-scorer of the 1960s. Inevitably therefore, all our conversations in the pub, out running, or on the drive to work centred on Donny and, when I could get a word in edgeways, the Swans.

With Mark living next-door-but-one, there was no way I could avoid Swans-duty. This was because every Saturday morning he would wait for me to appear and then taunt me about being a 'part-timer, lad' if I even remotely suggested that I wasn't going to drive to Swansea to watch a game against Rochdale. It never occurred to me to ask him why he wasn't heading to Carlisle to watch Donny that day.

All this meant that when I later moved to Newcastle and then Rugby I would go on to auto-pilot and travel to watch the Swans if they were playing anywhere within a radius of about 200 miles. Sadly, because the team was then doing so badly this gave me an unwanted introduction to the cathedral towns and backwaters of provincial England: York,

NUNEATON BOROUGH A.F.C. (1991)
MANOR PARK, BEAUMONT ROAD,
NUNEATON CV11 5HD. (0203) 385738

MATCH TICKET

F.A. CUP 1st ROUND REPLAY v SWANSEA CITY
at Manor Park, Nuneaton – Tuesday, 23rd Nov. 1993
Kick-off 7.30p.m.

£6.00 STANDING. HOME SUPPORTERS ONLY

02865

YOUR ARE ADVISED TO TAKE UP YOUR
POSITION 30 MINUTES BEFORE KICK-OFF
THIS PORTION TO BE RETAINED

TICKET DESIGN AND PRINT – CONTINUOUS FORMS SUPPLY (0533) 340477

Nuneaton away in 1993: an absolute bloody nightmare. I'm still in recovery

Hartlepool, Darlington, Donny, Mansfield, Bury, Rochdale, Lincoln, Cambridge, Notts County, Scunthorpe and so on.

At first these were solo ops, but over time a strong bond was established with fellow sufferers who I would recognise lurking about on the god-forsaken streets of some dreadful place in the middle of nowhere: Huw Richards, Peter and Bethan Charles, Clive Hughes and his boys (now men), Len Margetson, Richard Lilicrap, Gareth Phillips, and I would like to say 'many others' but of course at times the Swans away support at midweek games was so small it could have fitted into the proverbial telephone box. Here I cast my mind back to a humiliating defeat at Beazer Homes League Nuneaton Borough in an FA Cup replay when I counted 23 Swans fans, all of whom had to endure the agonies of extra-time and a missed penalty by super Johnny Cornforth on a bitterly cold and foggy November evening.

Very occasionally there were good times and there were plenty of laughs, mainly about how completely hopeless and futile it all was. On one notable occasion I took four non-Swans teacher friends to Notts County to see a midweek game: Peter Dewey aka Kenny Dewhurst, Phil Rosser aka Doss, a bemused New Zealander, Murray Owles, and Mike Gibbons who, inevitably, is known as 'Funky' (younger readers

17

will have to ask about this). For a week beforehand I gave this game a big build-up, telling them all how good the team was, and that they should look out for the likes of Paul Raynor and Steve Thornber. All I got in return were raised eyebrows and semi-polite smiles. In the event, and quite inevitably, the big night was a disaster. The Swans lost 2-1, it was bitterly cold (again), and the hundred or so away fans were outnumbered by heavily tooled-up riot police. Doss described it as 'quite possibly the worst night of my life', and it was almost as bad for manager Ian Evans, who was sacked a week later. The only shaft of light arose from the fact that, for reasons known only to themselves, the police took one look at us and insisted that we sit among the home fans in a rickety old stand that had wooden seats and flooring. Before long, those fans were stamping their feet and chanting 'County, County!' Doss thought that they were giving a nice warm Nottingham welcome to Mike Gibbons, who they had obviously recognised, so he encouraged us all to respond with our own chant of 'Funky, Funky!' This lasted almost ninety minutes and the bemused County fans were not at all sure what to make of it. The police looked on, truncheons at the ready.

By my mid-forties, I was beginning to concede very reluctantly that the call from the Swans would never come, even though I was still infinitely more talented than some of the donkeys who were sent out to graze on the Vetch Field during the 1980s and 1990s. For some reason, Aidan Newhouse comes to mind at this point. I had to find something else to do with my life, so I became a professor of History, and in 2007 Leicester University gave me a free transfer and I was snapped up by Swansea University, thus ending an exile in England that had lasted for almost thirty years.

So, I was home – but was I happy? Not really. Why not? In large part, it was because, as a Swans fan, until around 2005 – and then only with the brief exception of the Toshack years of 1977-82 – I had only ever experienced the grim inevitability of false dawns, failure, and misery by the bucket-load. This means that even though the Swans are now riding high in the Premier League, my default emotional position is that things are always about to go horribly wrong, and a run of defeats will lead to relegation, followed by further relegations, and then bankruptcy. Before you can say 'Tony Petty', we will be back playing Mansfield and having to put up with the internet ramblings of 'Mad Stag' and his ilk.

Indeed, I have always tended to take a dark view of the Swans, despite my devotion to them, as you can see from the following piece I wrote in 1999, which originally appeared in Keith Haynes' excellent book, *Come on Cymru 2000!* At the time I wrote it, the outlook for the Swans was very bleak and it seemed that things could never get better. Now, thankfully, the picture has switched to glorious Technicolor but back then it was monochrome.

CLOUDS OF DARKNESS, CLOUDS OF DESPAIR: KEEPING A WEATHER EYE ON SWANSEA CITY

Perhaps it is because the Swan, by nature, lives in a watery home; perhaps it is because Alan Curtis once walked on water; or perhaps it is because Harry Griffiths and John Toshack performed the most unlikely miracle and turned the murkiest of waters into the sweetest-tasting wine. Whatever the reason, Swansea City, in my mind, will always be associated with close encounters of the very wettest kind. To put it at its most simple: think Swans, think rain; think Vetch, think clouds of darkness and despair.

I am sure that I am not alone in taking a view of the Swans which charts the club's fortunes over the last thirty years or so in terms of weather patterns and atmospheric conditions in south-west Wales, the rain capital of Britain. Others of course have sought their explanations and patterns elsewhere. I remember one fanzine article which argued with great conviction that the team's league position always bore an exact correlation to the meat content of the pasties on sale at the Vetch (bring back the bakers Davies of Mumbles, all is forgiven); and there are those who suggest that the lamentable performance of successive generations of PA announcers lies at the very heart of all the club's problems over the years.

But I have long taken the view that any follower of Swansea Town or City is quite capable, like me, of having water on the brain. This is because our snapshot images and memories of the Vetch Field are more often than not shaped by recollections of games played out against a background of damp, dismal, windswept days and nights. Drizzle drifts past floodlight pylons across a quagmire pitch and into the faces of the poor deluded fools who sit in the East Stand in the mistaken belief that they are somehow going to find shelter from the elements. Water cascades down the dolls' house roof of the Centre Stand, falling past broken guttering and eventually forming glistening pools on the red shale running track.

On the pitch, white shirts turn brown, and would-be tacklers slither from the turf into advertising hoardings. The Vetch, living up to its name, slowly becomes a muddy, churned-up vegetable patch. And all the time, silently and out of sight, the puddle that always forms between the gateposts at the exit from the North Bank grows into an enormous lake which lies ready to claim hundreds more shuffling, grumbling victims who have not yet mastered the art of the thirty-foot leap from a standing start.

The Vetch: rain capital of south Wales

Tosh, who masterminded the Golden Years and even fixed the weather

No doubt I look back through mist-tinted glasses, but the only break in this thirty-year rainy season came when the Swans were taking flight in Division One, and game after game seemed to be played out in front of shirt-sleeved crowds in warm conditions and glorious sunshine. Alan Curtis destroyed Leeds in cricketing weather; Robbie James advanced on a retreating Spurs defence on a balmy late-summer evening; and Gary Stanley launched a thirty-yard missile of a shot into the Manchester City net in the bright spring sunshine. Maybe I have now wallowed in the nostalgia brought about by too many video re-runs of 'Swansea City: The Golden Years', but I am convinced that not a drop of rain fell on south-west Wales between August 1981 and May 1982. Tosh even fixed the weather. Golden years and golden days, but then someone switched the lights off again.

Contrast all this with times before and since, and think of Hull City, Rotherham United, Workington Town and Doncaster Rovers. The storm clouds gather in the mind, the outlook darkens, and it begins to rain. To the surface rise mildewed memories of bleak days, with little entertainment and not much hope. For me, the Vetch Field has become a theatre of wet dreams (no crude pun intended), and an even wetter reality.

The games that stick in the memory are those which were played out against a dark background of hail, snow, and torrential rain, and at times the only missing climatic ingredients were thunder and lightning above Townhill. Such fixtures that are perhaps easiest to recall are some of the biggest post-Toshack occasions: the Bournemouth 'rebirth' game of 1986; the West Brom play-off match; and most recently of course the West Ham cup replay. All were viewed through a watery curtain.

But there are hundreds of others – routine league fixtures – lurking in the recesses of all of our minds. Conjure them up for yourself and see. The away day, too, is now routinely an open-terraced, feet-numbing, rain-sodden, pointless experience which defies rational explanation to family, friends, and colleagues. Deeply etched on my soul is the 6-0 hammering on a glistening, sodden pitch on a dismal Darlington day. 4-0 or 5-0 down at half-time, we were awarded a penalty, only for Colin Pascoe to put the ball not only over the bar, but out of the ground as well. Only last season, a 4-1 reverse in driving rain at Cambridge was partially enlivened by the fact that there was so much mud on offer for players and spectators alike that Tony Bird felt obliged to present some of it to a linesman from a range of ten yards or more.

And Hartlepool, Hartlepool, Hartlepool. If only I could sing with some conviction of the Swans: 'You are my sunshine, my only sunshine, you make me happy when skies are grey . . .' Unfortunately, I can't ever quite bring myself to do it.

It was not always like this. Earliest memories of Swansea Town and the Vetch Field conjure up images of vivid colours, brightness, action, speed and, above all, a rich green pitch. Catching a first glimpse of the seemingly expansive playing surface, with the tinny strains of 'The Woody Woodpecker Song' playing in the background, was a defining, breathtaking moment, and even now the sight of the pitch still has the capacity to quicken the pulse and raise expectations at ten to three on a Saturday afternoon.

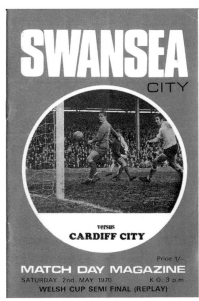

A programme from the 1969-70 season. A crowd of 20,479 saw this game, which the Swans lost 0-2. It was at this game that I experienced crowd trouble at close quarters for the first time. Not a happy experience for a ten-year-old

Unfortunately, however, the colour and brightness did not last. They first disappeared, temporarily, during the late sixties when the straw bales stored, quite bizarrely and recklessly, underneath the North Bank caught fire, and smoke billowed across the ground, obscuring pitch and stands alike. The crowd, cheerfully unaware that they were now standing on top of a potential towering inferno, provided an appropriate accompanying chorus of 'Swansea Town is burning down'.

But the clouds closed in permanently a short time later, when I entered into a completely unfamiliar, bleak world. This was not yet the long, dark tunnel of adolescence, in which inexplicable things happened, such as the exchange of two hundred Swans programmes for a couple of Barclay James Harvest albums (no excuses, but this was the early 1970s, when strange things happened to all of us). Rather this was a glamour-free world of lower division soccer entirely devoid of any colour and light.

The Vetch in the late 1960s, taken from the top tier of the 'Double Decker': a home from home

The Vetch. My spot (more or less) on the North Bank

The entry into this black hole occurred in March 1970 when, touched by promotion fever, I attended a midweek fixture against the late, lamented Bradford Park Avenue. What was unusual about this occasion (a 5-0 victory with Herbie Williams scoring a hat-trick) was that I did not sit in my usual spot on the low wall that runs in front of the North Bank. Instead, an accompanying uncle took me for the first time into the upper tier of the Double Decker stand, where spectators sat on bench seats and stamped their feet on a worryingly shaky wooden floor. This produced the disorientation that always accompanies such a move away from familiar spectating territory, but it also gave me my first 'aerial' view of a pitch which had been saturated by the constant heavy rain which continued to sweep in from the sea during the game.

Having been used to watching proceedings from a position level with, or even below, the playing surface, and always finding myself looking up into the bright floodlights, it came as something of a shock to realise that things were not as they had always seemed. The centre of the pitch itself resembled a swamp, with patches of mud joining together large pools of standing water. In fact the only evidence of any grass at all was to be found on the flanks patrolled by Carl Slee and Vic Gomersall (who surely must have possessed the deepest chest and thickest thighs of any of the players who ever turned out at the Vetch). The proceedings were played out in a murky semi-darkness that was so gloomy that it was easy, indeed fascinating, to watch the near-constant lighting and re-lighting of matches and cigarettes by fans standing on the North Bank.

Len Allchurch in action during a pre-season friendly against Accra Hearts of Oak in 1970. Photoshop ain't what it used to be

Although I was to return to my position on the North Bank for the next match, the effect of that visit to the Double Decker was to remain with me long after details of the game itself disappeared from view. Against the prevailing seventies trend, the Vetch was transformed from a colour set into black and white, and it is the watery, monochrome images that are now fixed in my mind. A few shafts of brightness are to be found, such as the pre-season friendly against Accra Hearts of Oak or some of the grotesque and garish programme cover designs and team strips that have been put before us over the years. But, 1981-82 apart, these are insignificant exceptions to the general rule which suggests that if you adopt the Swans as your team you must also prepare to take on the weather and the forces of darkness which can combine to do some very funny things to your mind.

It would be reassuring to believe that these dark Swansea clouds at least had some sort of silver lining within them. But they appear to have a Silver Shield instead and, as close observers of the Vetch Field barometer will tell you, this is not quite the same thing. Oh well, it looks like rain again.

FROM THE VETCH TO THE LIBERTY:
A HOME FROM HOME?

When I wrote the previous piece in 1999, few people could have predicted the traumas and problems that would be experienced by the Swans over the next four years or so. As we have seen, I have always been a miserable sod, but I really did have plenty to be miserable about between 1999 and 2003 despite the false dawn offered by winning the Third Division Championship in 2000.

The Swans had suffered severe financial problems before: in the late sixties, mid-seventies, and, most spectacularly, during the mid-eighties when the gates of the Vetch were locked and Doug Sharpe had to plead the club's case in the High Court. Then in the mid-nineties there had been the madness associated with a 'take-over' by the 'millionaire tycoon' Michael Thompson, whose master plan was to appoint as manager someone (I can't bring myself to write his name) who coached Cradley Town Youth and had no experience of professional football whatsoever.

But none of this prepared us for the meltdown that happened when, like a hot potato, the ownership of the Swans passed from Silver Shield to Ninth Floor to Mike Lewis and then to Tony Petty. The club was stripped to the bone and publicly humiliated, and the only good to come out of this sorry saga was that the energies of some of the most committed fans were gradually channelled into the formation of a Supporters' Trust.

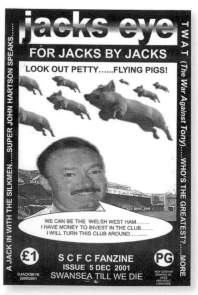

The War Against Tony Petty

28

The forced ejection of Petty from the club was a protracted and bloody affair, resembling a shoot-out in a spaghetti Western, at the end of which it was the Magnificent Seven who were left standing: Huw Jenkins, Martin Morgan, David Morgan, Leigh Dineen, Brian Katzen, John van Zweden, Steve Penny, Don Keefe, Gwilym Joseph, and Mel Nurse, ably assisted by the combative solicitor Tim Jones. Okay, that should read Magnificent Eleven, which does at least rhyme with Seven, and my sincere apologies go to the many others I have left out.

But, alas, the warm glow caused by the triumph over Petty soon disappeared as the team put together by the player-manager and all-round good guy Nick Cusack stumbled to the very bottom of the Football League for the first time in the club's history. This was serious, and Nick had to go. He was sacked just before a wretched game at Boston, and some of us who were at York Street on that dismal September evening spotted the arrival of would-be managerial replacements Brian Flynn and

The Vetch in 1990. I know that the crowds were small back then but this is ridiculous

Kevin Reeves. Someone (I can't remember who) persuaded Peter Charles to place a note under a windscreen wiper on Flynny's car. That scribbled note, which the new manager clearly could not read and threw away, was short and to the point: 'Good luck Brian. You're going to need it'.

As it happened, Flynn and Reeves did have the necessary luck, but I just wish that they hadn't waited until the last game of the season to find it during that pulsating, heart-stopping 4-2 victory over Hull City, a win that was (just) sufficient to keep the Swans up and send Exeter down through the trap door. Even professors ran on to the Vetch Field pitch that day.

Throughout this turbulent period, there had been talk of a new stadium being built for the Swans to replace the now seriously dilapidated and decaying Vetch. Silver Screen – or was it Ninth Floor? – had announced grandiose plans, but it was only in 2003-04 that a council-funded project slowly began to turn a pipe dream into reality.

Remarkably, as the plans for a new stadium at Morfa were being drawn up and implemented, the team's fortunes took a turn for the better, first under Flynn and then under Kenny Jackett who secured a promotion to Division Two before suffering an agonising Division One play-off defeat against Barnsley the following season. By the time the Swans moved into the imaginatively named 'New Stadium' in the early summer of 2005, there was a mood of optimism in the air. These were the Trundle Years, and we began to trundle along quite happily for once.

They say that the three most traumatic events in a person's life are bereavement, divorce, and moving home. Many fans were certainly upset about leaving the Vetch and there was plenty of emotion evident when the Swans defeated Shrewsbury 1-0 in the last league game, with Adrian 'Forbesey' Forbes smashing the winning goal past Joe Hart who, at the time of writing, is one of the best goalkeepers in the world. Again, professors ran on to the pitch at the end of the game, and on this occasion they ran off it again with clumps of Vetch Field turf in their pockets.

I certainly hated the whole process of leaving the Vetch behind. We had long comforted ourselves by saying 'It might be a dump but at least it's our dump.' Now we were moving to a new, sparkling stadium

which the club did not actually own. But Huw Jenkins had absolutely no sympathy for sentimentalists and softies like me. He was adamant that the club could not progress while it was locked into a broken-down ground in the Sandfields. 'What has history ever done for us?' he asked. As a professional historian it pains me to say this, but he was absolutely right, and almost from the moment that the Swans played their first league game at the new stadium against Tranmere they have experienced success and upward mobility.

So, the Liberty might be a nightmare to get to, and to get away from; the PA might be both deafening and incomprehensible; the East Stand catering might be terrible; and the whole place might lack warmth and identity; but at least the team has been winning and (mostly) sweeping all before it.

But I still miss the Vetch, and it pained me deeply to see it left overgrown with weeds and slowly rotting away. Eventually it was demolished and, quite appropriately, it became a vegetable patch once again, just as it had been during the 1870s when it had been thickly sown with 'vetch' and other plants. I suppose I should be pleased about this rebirth but when driving along Oystermouth Road, I do still miss seeing the floodlight pylons looming above the tightly packed houses, right at the heart of the community in which the Swans were so deeply embedded. But that is probably why I am a historian and not the proud chairman of Wales' first Premier League football club.

HEROES:
CLOSE ENCOUNTERS OF THE SWANS KIND

Sitting in the Liberty for the first time was a weird experience. My team was playing at 'home' but the surroundings were not familiar, and I lacked the usual points of reference: floodlight pylons, the Mel Nurse Bar, and the Black Hole of Calcutta that was the men's toilet behind the North Bank. Worst of all, though, I was sitting down, which I had almost never done at a game before. The next thing you know I'll be eating a prawn sandwich.

As I sat there rather uncomfortably, my mind wandered back to the Vetch and I thought about all those players I had seen over the years, very few of whom would ever grace the Liberty turf in a proper game. They were now consigned to a distant past, the sepia-print past of the Vetch. In particular, I thought of my heroes, some of whom I had actually met.

Carl Slee

Carl is notable because he was the first Swans player who ever spoke to me. He played in the first Swans team I watched during the late 1960s. With a shock of blond hair in a Beatles-style cut, he was a slim, youthful full-back who was very different from his counterpart on the other flank, Vic Gomersall. Vic, who had been at Manchester City, was a barrel-chested, no-nonsense tackler who was the epitome of intimidating muscular aggression and made barn-storming runs down the touchline. Carl, on the other hand, was finding his way in the game but was clearly very comfortable on the ball. He also appeared to be a little diffident and perhaps too respectful of some of his less skilful lower league opponents.

Carl was certainly polite, as I found during one game when I was in my customary position, perched on the little wall next to the shale running

The Swans squad of 1970-71. A favourite team, with Carl Slee third from the right in the back row. Vic Gomersall is sitting at the right-hand end of the second row from the front. Herbie 'Herbie is the greatest' Williams is standing next to Mel Nurse at the right-hand end of the row behind

track that ran along the length of the pitch in front of the North Bank. This was a precarious spot because there was a four- or five-foot drop behind us, but it allowed a legion of small boys to be within touching distance of both the action and the players. There was always a bit of a scramble when the ball went out of play as we fought to get hold of it and hand it back to the player preparing to take a throw-in. Only once did I ever manage to get hold of the ball, and I threw it to Carl who said 'Thanks'. That was it, but it was enough. One of my heroes had spoken. To me.

I have since met Carl on one or two occasions when I have gone to one of his shops, which is located a stone's throw away from the Vetch. He still looks as youthful and fit as he did then, and he is still just as modest and polite. A real hero. And a talking one at that.

Leighton James in full flight in September 1981. After Leighton hit the deck, Steve Perryman of Spurs went berserk and was booked. Leighton was then pelted with coins thrown by Spurs fans who chanted 'Cheat, cheat!' Leighton got up and gave a cheeky grin. The Swans won 2-1

Leighton James

Like me, Leighton went to Gowerton Grammar School, but he was a good few years ahead and when I entered the first form he had already signed for Burnley, which was then a top club in the top division. During the summer term he must have had a bit of time on his hands, because he used to come back to school to help out Robert Evans with the cricket coaching. This meant that during the first-year cricket trials, conducted on an uncut wicket behind the Chemistry lab, I found myself facing Leighton, who came in to bowl at me off a full run that seemed to rival in length that of John Lever, the Essex pace man. I suspect that Leighton has always been ferociously competitive and unlikely to take any prisoners, especially if they are weedy 11-year-olds. Consequently my participation in the trial lasted only one ball, and as I surveyed the wrecked stumps behind me, Leighton wheeled away, celebrating as though he had just bowled Ian Chappell to clinch The Ashes. Of course, he won't remember this, but the episode confirmed my lifelong status as a cowardly number eleven batsman whose instinctive first movement is always towards square leg. Thanks, Leighton.

Robbie James

During the run-up to the Capital One Cup final I was asked, out of the blue, to write a short piece for the British Library's 'Untold Lives' blog. The piece I wrote on Robbie James is reproduced below. It prompted some great responses from Tim Bowen, John Conibear, and Huw Richards, and these can be found on the British Library website in the 'Untold Lives' blog section for February 2013.

'King' Robbie James (1957-1998)

Searching for connections between Swansea City football club and Bradford City in the week before the Capital One Cup final at Wembley has not been a difficult task. This is because lots of players, and indeed one manager (Terry Yorath), have been employed by both clubs over the years. At first I was tempted to write about the tragic life of Alan Davies, once a teenage FA Cup winner with Manchester United, who

King Robbie James. They don't make men or moustaches like this any more

A young Robbie clocks up 100 games for the Swans

committed suicide while at Swansea in 1992. But in the end I just had to plump for Robbie James, one of the few footballers who fully deserve to be described as a legend, a term that is so often misused and abused when applied to sportsmen and women.

It has to be said that any non-aficionado of the beautiful game reading this will probably never have heard of Robert Mark James. But rest assured, the life of Robbie James is most certainly not an 'untold life' in south-west Wales, because Robbie was a driving force in the remarkable Swansea team of the late 1970s and early 1980s, which rose from the bottom of the Football League to the very top. Born near Swansea, he – along with Alan Curtis, Jeremy Charles, Wyndham Evans, and Nigel 'Speedy' Stevenson – was one of the local heroes we could all identify with and pin our hopes on. A barrel-chested attacking midfielder with a thunderous shot, he dominated the centre of the mud-heap pitch at the dilapidated Vetch Field, home of the Swans.

Robbie made 483 appearances for the Swans in two spells between 1973 and 1990. He scored 118 goals and won 47 international caps for Wales. But that is not all. In total, he made an astonishing 783 league appearances for various clubs over the course of a career that lasted for more than twenty years, and this included playing 89 games for Bradford City between 1990 and 1992. Unfortunately, though, he also inexplicably went over to the dark side in 1992-93 when he played 51 games for Cardiff City. When I heard the dreadful news that Robbie had signed for the Bluebirds (or are they Redbirds? Who knows?), I remember thinking, 'Say it ain't so, Robbie.'

After retirement from full-time professional soccer, Robbie played for several non-league teams in south Wales before becoming player-manager of Llanelli AFC. Tragically, but in some ways fittingly, Robbie collapsed and died while playing for Llanelli in 1998. The Half-Moon pub in Llanelli was renamed 'The Robbie James', and recently a bust of him was unveiled at the Liberty Stadium, the shiny new home of the now Premier League Swans.

The King shortly before his death, playing in a charity march for Showbiz Rangers

By all reports, Robbie was a cheerful, modest man, who sported a trademark 1970s moustache and had a genuine passion for the game he graced so wonderfully well. I only met him once, in a crowded bar during the early 1990s. As always happens when I am in the presence of one of my sporting heroes, I immediately lost the power of speech and started gaping at him like a goldfish. Recognising the difficulty I was in, Robbie leaned towards me, quietly said 'Alright, pal?', and shook my hand.

Quite simply, Robbie James was a class act, and is still much missed.

Alan Curtis

'Curt' is my all-time, number-one Swans hero. I have never met him or spoken to him, even though I wrote a tribute to him in the programme for his testimonial match against Fulham a few years back. I have actually been in his company once or twice, but on each occasion I learned that in the presence of a true Swans legend, I cannot even communicate a simple 'hello'. This is incredibly embarrassing and strange because I earn a living from talking to people, so I am seeking medical advice for this condition, which is known at acute Swanophobia. Apparently there is no known cure for it.

Alan Curtis signs for another team in south Wales. What on earth is there to smile about?

Told you! Curt soon turns to drink and religion

Wyndham Evans: the second hardest player ever to play for the Swans

Nigel Stevenson: Speedy by nature and Speedy by name (*sic*)

Wyndham Evans and Nigel 'Speedy' Stevenson

Much the same thing has happened with Wyndham and 'Speedy' as has always happened with 'Curt', but on one occasion when I met the two of them together after a game at the Liberty I did manage to overcome the 'Shit, it's a hero/legend' barrier and blurt out a few words. Unfortunately, on this occasion it involved me informing Wyndham authoritatively that he is the 'second hardest player ever to play for the Swans'. The shocked look on Speedy's face said it all, not least when I then revealed that in my expert opinion, the hardest player of all time was undoubtedly Wilfie Milne, who had played the last of his 587 games in 1937, twenty-two years before I was born. To be fair, both Speedy and Wyndham put up with this very well indeed, and they very patiently and politely listened to my ramblings. In fact, Wyndham was so good about it all that it is hard to believe that he is a Turk.

39

Mel Nurse

It was a similar story with Mel, who I met at the launch of the biography of Ivor Allchurch written by Peter Stead and the much-missed David Farmer. I found myself in a corner with Mel and managed to blurt out that he had been the captain of the first Swans team I ever saw. Casting my mind back I can see him now: a tall, commanding, swarthy figure, as hard as nails (but not as hard as Wyndham) in his all-white kit, looking for all the world as though he was playing for Real Madrid. Now, I am taller than Mel but I told him 'Mel, you looked like a giant'. He looked at me as though I was mad, thought about it, and said 'Yes', before adding 'but you was only nine at the time'. I could only agree that this was a fair point.

Mel Nurse in 1971: a giant

Even so, Mel is still a giant in my book because it seems crystal clear to me that, without his critical interventions over the years, there would be no Swansea City Football Club at all. How sad it is then, that on the day of the club's supreme achievement against Reading in the Championship play-off final, Mel was not at Wembley but at the bedside of his very ill wife, who was in Singleton Hospital. Sad, but typical of a man who always seems to have recognised that although Swansea Town/City Football Club is at the very core of his being, there is in fact much more to life than football. This is something that some of us would do well to remember from time to time.

Chris Coleman

Away at Scarborough in September 1986, I was with my mate, the diehard Liverpool fan Roy Firth, when we were given the only 'comps' I have ever received, and to our astonishment we found ourselves sitting next to Doug Sharpe in the front row of the directors' box. At half-time, as we (and we alone) tucked in to the free sarnies and cakes in the boardroom, I became vaguely aware of someone hovering next to us. I turned to find a seventeen-year-old Chris Coleman standing there in his Swans tracksuit. Chris had made his debut in the first game of the season against Stockport but, although he wasn't in the squad for the game against newly-promoted Scarborough, who were managed by Neil Warnock, he had obviously travelled with the team. Now he was holding out a polystyrene cup and he asked, 'Boys, is there any sugar? We've got none in the dressing room.' Without turning away from the freebies, we were happy to oblige, blissfully unaware of course that we were in the presence of a future star player and manager of Wales.

Chris Coleman: just find me some sugar!

Future manager of Wales

Swansea Town Reserves, 13 August 1949. Tom Kiley is in the centre of the front row

Tom Kiley

The only Swan I have ever spoken to at any great length is one who I never saw play. About fifteen years ago, I started collecting material for a history of the Swans that was to be written using only the words of fans and players. As part of this ill-fated project which never saw the light of day, I arranged to interview Tom Kiley, who had been at the heart of the great Swans team of the mid-1950s. Indeed, any of the generation of supporters who revered the team that contained Ivor, Cliff Jones, Harry Griffiths, Mel Charles, Terry Medwin and the rest will tell you that, were it not for Tom Kiley's ultimately career-ending injury picked up in training only days after a superb 2-1 victory over Liverpool, the Swans, who were then top of the table, would definitely have been promoted to the top division in 1955-56. After Tom crocked his knee, it was then more or less downhill all the way for the Swans for the rest of the season and, indeed, for about a dozen seasons after that.

As it was, Tom turned out to be a real gentleman and a brilliant interviewee, who recalled every aspect of his career in great detail. He gave up his time generously and answered my questions patiently and at considerable length. The only thing that perplexed me was that Tom had asked that the interview be conducted in the lounge of the rugby club-house at St Helen's, where he exchanged banter with the likes of Scott Gibbs and Arwel Thomas. When I asked him about this, Tom told me that for many years he had been a follower of the All-Whites and he now organised all the away travel for the supporters' club. I wondered about his current connections with the Swans, and he replied that he had been to the Vetch only once since the end of playing career over forty years earlier. He revealed that he had hated playing at home, where he could hear every criticism thrown in his direction from the stands and banks, and he especially resented it whenever he had been accused of 'not trying'. Later he had become appalled by hooliganism and foul language and he simply could not bring himself to watch the Swans, or indeed any other soccer. So instead, he devoted his retirement to rugby and cricket. How sad is that? And what a loss to the game that was, because Tom was undoubtedly one of the most articulate and sharp-minded people I have ever met.

Julian Alsop: 'Use your pace, Alsop!'

Julian Alsop

By coincidence, the lounge at St Helen's was the scene of an encounter with the Swans striker Julian Alsop who, it is fair to say, was effective but limited in the very solid and well-organised side that won the Division Three Championship under John Hollins in 1999-2000. 'Big Jules' was very tall and good in the air, and thus was a perfect target man rather than a goal-scorer. The fact that he scored three league goals in 37 appearances that season in a title-winning side says it all really, but he was a whole-hearted trier and the crowd appreciated the key part he played in the functional but hardly thrilling Hollins system. It is also fair to say that Julian was not blessed with a great turn of speed, and could perhaps best be described as 'lumbering', which is why Peter Stead's exasperated, top-volume cries of 'Come on Alsop, use your pace' from the North Bank were always guaranteed to bring the house down.

Anyway, during one of the magnificent fundraising race-night events organised for the fledgling Supporters' Trust by Gary Martin, I staggered towards the gents. While washing my hands I turned round to find that 'Big Jules' had appeared and was approaching the urinal. Before I could say anything, one of my fellow revellers shouted, 'Oi Alsop, be careful – you'll probably miss.' To be fair, the striker took it very well, but looking back, and in view of what happened later on in his career, I am glad for the sake of the toilet-humourist that there were no bananas in the vicinity.

As a footnote, I noticed that Julian recently ended his career playing for Carmarthen Town, where again he had provided sterling service as a non-goal-scoring centre-forward.

Matthew Bound

Matthew was a really good centre-back who was a team-mate of Julian Alsop. Unfortunately, he left the Swans under something of a cloud when the club melted down financially in 2001. This cloud appeared because he claimed monies that were owed to him by the club and as a result some fans denounced him as a 'greedy b*****d'. This begs the obvious question: how many of us would not try to recover money owed to us by an employer whose gross financial mismanagement had caused the firm to go bust? Hmm, thought so, but I suppose it is inevitable that some fans apply a very different set of rules when their club is in the frame and likely to become extinct.

Matthew Bound: a good player and a good bloke

I met Matthew a couple of years ago as we were both waiting to get on a coach to take us to the annual rugby match between Cardiff University and Swansea University that now takes place at the Millennium Stadium. Nobody else appeared to know who Matthew was, so I said hello, and we then chatted all the way to the game. I learned more in an hour about the realities and anxieties of being a professional footballer than I could have learned from a thousand books. 'Boundy', who now has a business in Mumbles, was great company and appears to be a decent touch-rugby player as well as a veteran soccer player. Indeed, he still looks as fit as he did when he lined up in one of my favourite Swans 'back fours' of Steve Jones-Jason Smith-Matthew Bound-Michael Howard.

THE EIGHT MOST IMPORTANT GAMES IN THE HISTORY OF THE SWANS

In the build-up to the Capital One Cup final against Bradford there was much talk in the press about this being the most important game in the club's history. With all due respect, this was nonsense, but it did get me thinking about those games that had been more important. I am with Alan Curtis on this one. He said that the cup final is the most significant game in the club's history but not the most important. I think I know what he means. Kind of.

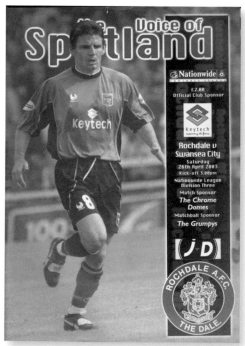

Rochdale away in 2003. The most important game in the club's history. Note the name of the match ball sponsor. We would all have been grumpy for the rest of our lives if we had lost that one

1. *Rochdale, away, 26 April 2002, won 2-1*

Without a victory in this game, the Hull game would have been irrelevant. If you were not at this game without a good excuse, you should be ashamed of yourself. The second half was almost unbearable, with Marc Richards going half the length of the field to score the winning goal about a minute after coming on as a substitute. Other highlights were the pre-match fish and chips, and watching a very embarrassed but obviously proud Alan Tate and his parents being applauded all the way back to their car after the game.

2. *Hull City, home, 3 May 2002, won 4-2*

Victory staved off relegation from the Football League. An unbelievably stressful and emotional day was made even more special by James Thomas' extraordinary hat-trick. This included a brace of penalties won by Leon Britton, who twice got into the opposition box, something that hasn't happened since. The survival campaign was masterminded by Brian Flynn and Kevin Reeves, and, on the field, key contributions were made by every single player, although Huw Richards always argues that the signing of Lenny Johnrose was probably the most important ever made by the club.

3. *Reading, Wembley, 30 May 2011, won 4-2*

Victory in the Championship play-off final took the Swans into the Promised Land of the Premier League. Scott Sinclair won plaudits for his hat-trick, but my men of the match (on the field) were Stephen Dobbie and Garry Monk. The latter's battling display convinced me that I should finally forgive him for the bizarre own goal he scored away at Lincoln in April 2005. This injury time OG was a hoofed slice into the top corner and condemned the Swans to a 1-0 defeat against their promotion rivals. The drive back home from Sincil Bank was one of the longest and most miserable I have ever experienced.

4. *Preston North End, away, 2 May 1981, won 3-1*

I am ashamed and embarrassed to say that, although I saw most games during that momentous season, I missed 'The Big One' when 10,000 Jacks descended on Deepdale to celebrate the win that took the Swans into the top division for the first time. My excuse: I was forced to sit a Part II History exam in Aberystwyth on the Saturday morning. I tried to get special permission from the Head of Department, Professor R.R. Davies, to attend the game, but he replied that by acceding to such a request he would be creating an 'unwelcome precedent'. He then rubbed salt into my gaping wound by telling me that he had watched the Swans in years gone by and was delighted that promotion was about to be clinched. So while my mate 'Scab', who had only ever seen three Swans games, enjoyed himself in the away end at Preston, I was patrolling the midfield for AFC Talbot-Neasden in the university intra-mural league, while at the same time listening to Ron Jones's BBC Wales radio commentary on a tiny transistor radio.

5. *Nottingham Forest, home, 16 May 2011, won 3-1*

This victory in the play-off semi-final clinched the Swans' place at Wembley, after an unbelievably good ten-man performance in the first leg which ended 0-0 at the City Ground. The highlights were Darren Pratley's final-minute goal scored from inside his own half, and the East Stand being shaken to its copper-bottomed foundations as the delirious fans jumped up and down. Even Martin Johnes stopped tweeting for a moment to join in.

6. *Bolton Wanderers, away, White Hart Lane, 27 March 1926, lost 0-3*

A hugely disappointing FA Cup semi-final defeat. John Conibear, who was born in 1925 and surely must have been at the game, tells me that there were not many Swans fans there because, during hard economic times, most were saving their money for what they believed would be an inevitable trip to the final at Wembley. He also reports that Garry Monk was a rock in defence in a team that contained the Swans' greatest striker, Jack Fowler.

7. *Preston North End, away, Villa Park, 14 March 1964, lost 1-2*

Another hugely disappointing FA Cup semi-final defeat. John Conibear, who must surely have been there, tells me that we woz robbed in a game played in front of 68,000 rain-sodden spectators. He also reports that Garry Monk was a rock in defence in a team that contained one of the Swans' greatest goalkeepers, Noel Dwyer, whose daughter Carol became a glamour model and then married the footballer Frank Worthington.

8. *Bradford City, Wembley, 24 February 2013 won 5-0*

The Capital One Cup final, 2013. Important, but not that important.

THE DIARY: ROAD TO WEMBLEY

MONDAY 18 FEBRUARY 2013:

IT'S IN THE DNA, OR:
SWANSEA CITY (ALMOST) RUINED MY LIFE

I was nine years old when I first sensed that other people thought there was something seriously wrong with me.

Every other Saturday I would leave the house wearing my prized black and white Swans scarf. Heading for Vetch Field, I would also clutch a wooden rattle, carefully inscribed with the words 'Herbie is the Greatest'. Yes, Herbie Williams really *was* that good.

But 'going down the Vetch' with my mate Nick was no easy operation. This was because always lying in wait for me was my nemesis, Great-Uncle Bertie, who had single-handedly defeated Hitler and still wore his old 53rd Welsh Division beret to prove it.

He seemed to spend his whole life leaning on the gate of his house next door, smoking his pipe and waiting for me to appear. On first catching sight of me he would spring into action and gleefully bellow at the top of his voice: 'What are you doing wasting your money on that bloody lot? Give it to me instead. You must be a bloody idiot!' and so on. Crushed, I would slink away to the bus stop, with his hoots of derision ringing in my ears.

And it got worse. My irritating little sister soon picked up on this, so much so that to this very day she still refers to me as 'The Moron'. This is nice, especially as I am now fifty-three and she is no longer quite so irritating. I'm sure she doesn't really mean it; or at least I hope she doesn't.

But they had a point. In the early 1970s, the Swans were in Division Three before things took a marked turn for the worse, and relegation was soon followed by near-bankruptcy. Swans fans were treated as though they were members of a leper colony, and as with all leper colonies, our numbers dwindled away every year.

Things were so bad that even I started to enjoy listening to Barclay James Harvest, a prog-rock band who specialised in doom-laden anthems about death and suicide.

After the all-too-brief dizzying rise and fall of the Swans during the Toshack era, normal service was resumed. Mockery and misery were served up in large doses as the penniless Swans lurched around the lower leagues like a drunken pantomime clown with his foot stuck in a bucket of custard.

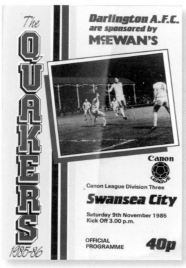

Darlington away in 1985: the lowest of many low points. The Quakers 6, The Swans 0. I was quaking for weeks after that one

Roary the Lion who (unwisely) went head-to-head with Peter Charles at Moss Rose in 2003

But I still went to the games, through thin and thinner, even though I had now 'grown up' and moved far away from Swansea.

So why did I do it? Why did a man who was seemingly sane and sensible [*Check this, please. Ed*] get up on a Saturday morning, ignore all other available entertainment options, and then drive 250 miles to Hartlepool, only to be rewarded with yet another dismal defeat for the men in white or, by now, some hideous orange and blue away kit?

I concede that it is very odd, not least because my personal list of Swans-related humiliations is an extremely long one, which should have persuaded me to throw in the towel by now.

There was the 6-0 hammering at Darlington, after which a police horse stepped on my foot. This truly dreadful day out begs many questions, the most notable of which is why on earth two police horses were required to control a crowd of 2,621.

Then there was the incident with the Macclesfield mascot, Roary the Lion, a heated altercation which almost ended in fisticuffs involving several other respectable members of the community (you know who you are).

And worst of all, there was the 1-0 defeat at Boston, after which the Swans slumped to the very bottom of the Football League for the first time ever. If that wasn't bad enough, I was booked for speeding on the way home, fleeing the scene of the crime, as it were. This meant that by the end of September 2002, I had more points on my driving licence than the Swans had on the board in the league table.

The only other time I have been stopped for speeding was on my way to a game against Scarborough. When I explained to the officer where I was going, his dead-pan response was: 'Then speeding really isn't necessary is it, sir?'

Of course, along with these agonies, there were occasional ecstasies, which perhaps made it all worthwhile. Great goals, unlikely comebacks, giants slain, and even promotions.

But it was also about something else – a sense of identity and belonging laced with the dark humour that emerges from within groups of people when they are conscripted into ultimately futile tasks. This produces vivid memories, not only of goals and players, but also of comedy moments, wisecracks, and perfectly delivered one-liners.

A single example will suffice.

On one occasion, a rag-bag collection of academics, pseudo-intellectuals, and other social misfits were gathered together in a small, grumbling huddle on the freezing terraces on the 'away end' at Rotherham (or was it Halifax?). Peter Stead, who in his own eyes at least is the greatest manager the Swans have never had, nodded in the direction of the nearest other Swans fan who was standing by himself about thirty yards away. 'Do you know who that is?' 'No. Who?' 'The Professor of Moral Philosophy at Columbia University.' After that, it somehow didn't seem to matter that the Swans lost 4-0.

But of course, it's all very different now. The Swans, once the modern-day equivalent of Fred Karno's Circus Army, have become the hottest ticket in town. They have also come to epitomise what every fan would want their football club to be.

They are a 'people's club', run by fans with the fans, and without a here today, gone tomorrow foreign owner (yet). They are a team that plays in a magnificently stylish and creative way. The players appear to be decent and humble, without any big-time Charlies among them. And the manager, the Great Dane, is a class act.

This suits us down to the ground, because Swansea people are modest people; indeed they are often far too modest for their own good. So there is no dim-witted boasting about being 'bigger than Barcelona' or indeed anyone else, although Swansea is indisputably bigger than Bonymaen. But the sweet irony of it all is that many onlookers now seem to believe that the Swans have in fact become the new Barcelona.

Looking back to the time when small groups of Swans fans trailed around the country like the remnants of a badly beaten rabble army, who could possibly have believed that this would ever happen? I certainly didn't.

As a historian by trade, I am certain of only one thing in life and that is that nothing is inevitable. In the not-too-distant future, there might well be a time when the Swans again have to sample the delights of lower league football. God forbid that such a terrible thing should ever happen.

I don't know what the programme and kit designers were on during the late 1980s and early 1990s but I want some of it

But if it is does, one thing is for sure: I'll be there. Because for some strange, unfathomable reason, it's in my DNA.

So, Great Uncle Bertie, wherever you might be, put that in your pipe and smoke it! And, as for you, sis, no, you can't have a ticket for Wembley!

TUESDAY 19 FEBRUARY:

WEMBLEY – IT'S DÉJÂ VU ALL OVER AGAIN

Some of us have been down this road before. Three times, in fact. And our record at Wembley is not a bad one. Played three, won two, lost one. But truth be told, I haven't enjoyed the experience.

And, if history really does repeat itself, I am not expecting to have a good time on Sunday. On balance, I would probably prefer an away game at Doncaster. But I suppose I'll just have to bite the bullet and get on with it.

So what's the problem? Why can't I just lighten up and enjoy the moment? The Swans. At Wembley. In the final.

It's because the previous three occasions have proved disappointing, deflating and stressful in equal measure.

The first trip to Wembley was in 1994 for the final of the Spud-u-like Trophy or some other such major cup final. I went with my mates Chunky, Kipper and Haemo. I was disappointed that I was the only one without a nickname, or perhaps the others were just kind enough not to tell me what it was.

It was also disappointing that Wembley Stadium – the Mecca of English football – turned out to be a run-down, dilapidated dump on a North London trading estate. So much for the romance of the cup.

We won 3-1 on penalties after extra time, and I was especially delighted for my favourite Swans manager of all-time, 'mad' Frankie Burrows. Frank was old-school, and always sported a trademark flat cap, which he probably wore to bed and eventually had to have surgically removed from his balding head. He was, though, a seriously good manager and I often wonder what he could have done with £20 million instead of the £20 in loose change that chairman Doug Sharpe gave him to spend on the team.

We celebrated the victory by dancing up and down in the gangways while singing the Roger Freestone song and manically waving our arms in the manner of our legendary keeper, who had just saved the final penalty. Roger, Roger; Roger, Roger; Roger; Roger; Freestone; Roger! (repeat ad nauseam; lyrics: Dai Smutto).

At least we won in 1994. Three years later we lost 1-0 to Northampton in the Division Three play-off final. This was a travesty, with the goal coming in the very last minute after (scandalously) a twice-taken free kick. What a load of cobblers.

I have erased most of that dreadful experience from my memory. But I do recall trudging back down Wembley Way to the tube station carrying an inflatable six-foot banana, which for reasons I can't recall was a must-have football accessory in those days.

I was overtaken by a large man carrying a huge inflatable shark. 'Cheer up, lads,' said a Cockney copper. Without looking up, my temporary companion replied, 'I'm gutted, he's gutted, even the ******* shark's gutted'. Only briefly did I wonder whether it is actually possible to gut an inflatable fish.

And so to May 2011 and The Really Big One. The Championship play-off final against Reading. As everyone knows, we won 4-2, entered the Promised Land, and the rest, as someone once said, is history. This should have been a happy, pleasant experience, as indeed it was for thousands, but instead it turned into one of the worst days of my life. I will spare you the grim details – I can already feel myself tensing up as I type – but suffice it to say that the day involved a 6.00am start to drive, not to Wembley, but instead to Hay-In-The-Middle-of-Nowhere where, at 9.00am, along with Peter Stead and Martin Johnes, I was participating in the Literary Festival (yeah, yeah, I know, but someone has to do it).

At 10.00am, after a sharply truncated debate about the place of history in modern

Peter Stead talks tactics: 'I want you all to pile forward and then just get the ball to Ivor.'

Welsh culture, we made a tyre-burning exit from Hay. As part of the master plan to avoid clogged-up country roads, we drove up the M5 then along the M42 south of Birmingham before picking up the M40 south to Bicester. As we passed Worcester and saw the sign pointing to 'Scotland and the North', Stead muttered quietly to himself: 'So the new Wembley was moved after all', at which point Johnes sat slumped silently in the back of the car.

After being stuck for ages in a traffic jam leading to a retail park on the outskirts of Bicester, we abandoned the car and hopped on a train to London, which soon filled up with noisy Reading fans, who eyed us with great suspicion. We eventually made it to Wembley with seconds to spare and arrived at our seats breathless, sweating, shaking and stressed-out, big-time.

Things were so bad that when the rampant Swans went 3-0 up, an ashen-faced and characteristically worrisome Stead actually said: 'I don't like the look of this. 3-0 is always a dangerous score line'. Around us, everyone was delirious with excitement but, as ever, Stead was right. When Reading pulled it back to 3-2, I thought that the three of us would suffer a collective heart attack. Then, instead of celebrating when Scott Sinclair

Wembley 1994: Super Johnny Cornforth (left) and Roger, Roger; Roger, Roger; Roger Roger; Roger Freestone

Wembley 1997: gutted, and I know exactly how he felt

wrapped things up with his second penalty, I was already worrying about how we would get back to bloody Bicester.

For some reason known only to himself, Robin Turner of the *Western Mail* thought that this was newsworthy, and he reported on our high-speed cross-country caper under the headline 'Three Professors in Mad Dash to Wembley'. Unfortunately, most people skim-read this as 'Three Mad Professors in Dash to Wembley', and as a result of subliminal word association, we have become known in some quarters as the 'Mad Professors'. Stead reports that people whom he doesn't know approach him regularly in Tesco or at high-level literary functions eager to ask him not about the Dylan Thomas Literary Prize that he runs, but whether he is one of the three Mad Professors. Actually, we don't mind this very much at all, but secretly, we refer to ourselves as the Three Stooges.

WEDNESDAY 20 FEBRUARY:

THE VIRTUAL WAITING ROOM

Long before the sweet moment of success in the League Cup semi-final against Chelsea, the minds of thousands of Swans fans had already turned to the logistics of how to get to Wembley for The Big One, the eighth most important game in the club's history.

As the rest of the world lost the plot and became momentarily obsessed with 'Ball-boy gate', elaborate plans were being hatched to secure a very large Jack Army presence in London NW1 on Sunday 24 February. All that was needed was for 36,000 people to sort out tickets and travel.

In theory this was simple, but in practice it proved to be an absolute nightmare. Friendships have been strained and stress levels have increased dramatically all over south-west Wales. Had we known this at the outset, would we have put ourselves through the wringer for the past ten days? Of course we would, because give a football fan a tantalising glimpse of whatever now passes for the twin towers of Wembley, and he or she just has to be there whatever the cost to personal health, bank balance, and sanity.

So when my mate Huw Morris casually suggested that it would be a good idea to order two coaches to convey the 'Jackademics' (geddit?) to Wembley, I didn't give the matter a second thought. We agreed that we would fill one coach each with academics and assorted hangers-on from Swansea University.

Now, on the face of it this should have been pretty straightforward, but given the nature of the great minds that are to be found in any university, it is an operation that is akin to herding cats, and pretty dysfunctional cats at that. Because, despite all their doom-laden warnings to feckless students about time management and planning ahead, many academics are in fact singularly incapable of following the simplest instruction or meeting a deadline.

So the straightforward request – tell me how many seats you want and bung a cheque in the mail – is disdainfully ignored, especially by those from Cardiganshire, thus leaving the personal finances of Bowen and Morris in utter disarray.

But this is nothing compared to the trial and tribulations of trying to buy tickets online in an attempt to avoid having to join a shuffling, grumbling, freezing-cold queue at the Liberty.

What on earth was I thinking of when I agreed to become 'lead purchaser' for a linked group of sixteen season-ticket holders? Little did I know that being bombarded by texts with the message 'Have you got them yet?' would have such a dramatic effect on my blood pressure.

As with over 10,000 other season tickets holders, at precisely 8.30am last Wednesday morning, I hit the 'buy tickets' button on the SCFC website . . . and absolutely nothing happened. That's not quite true, because a message informed me that I was now in a 'virtual waiting room'. Three hours later I was tearing my virtual hair out, and the tension was mounting by the minute.

I was eventually called in from the virtual waiting room, and the whole transaction was completed in about fifteen seconds. In triumph, I sent out a text with the good news. But instead of receiving congratulations for my dogged determination under fierce pressure, I received a barrage of urgent questions: 'What row am I in?' 'Are we together?' 'Am I at the end of the row?' All from people with far too much time on their hands.

Later, I met with Siân Williams of the South Wales Miners Library. Usually calm and unflappable, Siân was edgy, drawn, and distracted, her mind clearly still trapped in the virtual waiting room. I don't know whether or not Siân smokes, but she looked like a woman in urgent need of a cigarette. We compared notes, as if in an attempt to outdo each other in a 'So when did you get yours?' competition. I beat her quite comfortably by more than an hour, but then she played her trump card by saying, 'Yes, but you didn't have Alun Burge standing behind you saying "'Ow you doin?'" every two minutes. Now that *is* stressful, and I conceded defeat.

But all's well that ends well. Tickets secured. Seats on coach booked. Tidy. Now all we have to do is sit back, relax, and enjoy it. Isn't it?

THURSDAY 21 FEBRUARY:

TALKING SWANS

During my lunch-break I forego my usual sherry and four-course lunch with the Academic Registrar and instead nip into to town to pick up the Jackademics T-shirts and flag I have ordered from Jon Price at Dorian Heel Bar ('Premier League Printing at its Very Best'). Jon has been doing a roaring trade in the build-up to The Final, but his shop in Oxford Street is unusually crowded today as fans pick up their essential accessories for Wembley.

In one corner of the shop is a small excited huddle of people all looking at something and taking photographs. What's going on? What can this be?

Ever the diligent researcher, I work my way into the crowd and find the object of all this close attention, but I am still none the wiser. People are gazing in awe and wonderment at something in a way that our ancestors would have done when they looked upon sacred religious bones or relics.

I can contain my curiosity no longer and ask quietly, 'What is it?' The awe-inspired, whispered response is 'It's Ashley Williams's wash-bag'.

Upon further close questioning, it seems that the wash-bag has been owned by Ashley since he was a teenager, and it has become a lucky charm.

Dorian Heel Bar: a Swans Emporium. 'Premier League Printing at its Very Best!'

Now, in preparation for the big day, it has been brought in so that the old, rusting zip can be replaced.

I am not sure that this is the time to be messing about with new zips which might upset the karma, but I am sure that Captain Ash knows what he is doing. I am too amazed even to take a photograph.

In the Heel Bar, as everywhere else, everyone's talking about them. And it. The Swans. The Final. On the bus, in the shop, in the market. Yadda, yadda; Leon, Leon; Michu, Michu; Wembley; Wembley.

Now I suppose I should be pleased about this. But instead, I find it grating, even irritating. I don't know why, but I suppose I rather enjoyed it when the Swans were a minority interest, an acquired taste, a passion that could not be talked about in public. As someone said to me rather smugly on my first day at Swansea University only five years ago, 'Oh, you won't find anyone here to talk with about the Swans. We're all Ospreys.'

How times have changed. Now the Ospreys barely rate a mention as all and sundry earnestly spend their coffee-break moments discussing Chico's ankle ligaments and the minutiae of Gerhard Tremmel's new contract. Oh yes, we're all members of the Jack Army now.

Which brings me very neatly to my dear little sister. Not so very long ago, she mocked me incessantly. 'You must be mad, you moron,' she would hoot derisively. 'What on earth are you doing driving all the way to Darlington/Scarborough/Hartlepool to watch that bunch of no-hopers? You idiot.'

She now claims (quite absurdly, of course) that this relentless verbal assault was simply her revenge for the fact that at the age of seven I had jabbed the sharp end of a cricket stump through every plastic window of her dolls' house. As if.

But these days, her conversation takes a very different turn as she muses whether 'we' should use a 4-5-1 formation with Pablo deployed in a floating role behind Michu.

Fair play, though, this is not idle chatter, because my sister and her lesser half have even joined a supporters group known as the West Swansea Plastics. Membership of this well-heeled posse is sharply defined. All are refugees from Ospreylia, own Labradors, and play a game called golf. And they just love the padded seats at the Liberty.

Now, none of this would matter at all were it not for the fact that my sister has in fact become much closer to the Swans than I could ever be. And this hurts. Badly.

How has this happened? Well, my sister just happens to work as a radiographer at a hospital in Swansea, and one of the very arduous duties she has to perform is to scan the injured body parts of footballers. So she meets the players on a regular basis, chats and jokes with them, and even asks them to undress for her. As a result, she has seen more footballers' groins than even the waggiest WAG.

Siân Roberts: a Plastic at Wembley. 'Hey, sis, the pitch is behind you and we're the ones in white.'

Of course, firm adherence to a strict code of professional conduct means that she never reveals the details of her work to me despite my best, and at times desperate, efforts to get the inside track. Instead she taunts me, knowing full well that since the age of eight I have had an insatiable appetite for all Swans-related info.

So imagine the agonies I go through when she reminds me that she is now so close to the Swans that she knows the colour of the underwear worn by every single player. She even reveals that one of them (Spanish of course) always turns up for a scan wearing a pair of skimpy pink briefs under his jeans, a regular occurrence that leads to standing-room only as nurses flock to the scanning room.

Knowing that she knows what I want to know but can never know, she exercises complete control in our relationship. And I have to admit that once – just once, mind – she stitched me up beautifully.

This was during the build-up to the Championship play-off final at Wembley two years ago when close attention was being paid to the state of captain Garry Monk's bad back. She could not resist telling me 'in strictest confidence' that our talisman would definitely miss the final and would probably never play again.

Within seconds I had texted everyone I knew with the msg 'Monkey out deffo'. My few remaining shreds of credibility were then comprehensively shot to pieces a few days later when Garry Monk not only led out the side at Wembley and raised the trophy, but produced a game-changing moment when he heroically flung himself and his bad back in front of a goal-bound pile-driver of a shot. Within seconds my ears were burning as my phone went into melt-down mode (as happened again a few weeks ago when Stead duped me into passing on the top-secret news that Didier Drogba had just signed for the Swans).

So, dear sister, enjoy your day out at Wembley with your prawn-sandwich-munching chums. Just remember one thing, though, as you look down on us from your hospitality box: we're the ones in white.

FRIDAY 22 FEBRUARY:

SWANSEA! OH SWANSEA!

Perhaps the most important part of the last-minute preparations for The Big Day has been sorting out the CD to play on the coach. Responsibility for this vital task has been given to Phil Roberts, an ageing rocker and David Byrne lookey-likey who works for the City and County of Swansea.

(Phil, if you are reading this, mate, get the cheque to me pronto or you and your mob are off the bus to be replaced by some of the West Swansea Plastics who have suddenly discovered my phone number.)

The only instruction I have given Phil is that there must be no renditions of 'Hymns and Arias' on our bus. This is because, with all due respect to Max Boyce, there is no place for this sentimental rugby dirge at a soccer match.

There is of course a time and a place for this exquisitely-crafted masterpiece, but, quite frankly, it is not at a Swans game. Some of the North Bankers of old must be turning in their graves every time they hear the wretched thing.

How has it come to this? How have we sunk so low as to appropriate an anthem from the 'handling code'? How have the witty, boisterous chants of yesteryear, such as that all-time classic, 'You're gonna get your ******* head kicked in', been replaced by a rugby song that reduces men of a certain age and size to tears?

Well, I know who is to blame and, yes, you've guessed it, it's those pesky West Swansea Plastics.

I can recall first hearing 'Hymns and Arias' only two years ago at the play-off semi-final home leg against Forest. And I can reveal exclusively that it was started in the West Stand by a certain consultant at Morriston Hospital who had had one too many white wine spritzers in the Platinum Lounge. This charlatan (and you know who you are) should have a football banning order imposed upon him. And then he should be deported back to Ospreylia, whence he came.

All of this means that on Sunday, if you listen very carefully, when 36,000 thousands Jacks are giving full voice to 'Hymns and Arias' you will hear someone trying to shut them up. That will be me. Why? Cos it's about 'istory, see.

Instead I will be attempting to start up some of the following favourites that will have been playing on the Jackademics buses on the way to Wembley. Just to get us in the mood, like.

'The Woody Woodpecker Song', first played over the PA system at the Vetch at the beginning of the 1948-49 season when the Swans won every league game bar one, which was a draw, and were promoted as champions to Division Two. The song was considered to be such a lucky omen that they were still playing it twenty-five years later, despite the fact that it was now having the opposite effect and the club was rooted at the bottom of Division Four.

My favourite North Bank chant of all time began with the words 'Zigger, Zagger; Zigger Zagger, Rah! Rah! Rah!' The rest is not suitable for a family audience, but you can probably work it out for yourselves. I found it absolutely hilarious when I was ten, and I'm really sorry, Vice Chancellor, but it still makes me laugh now.

A collection of old hits including Slade's 'Run, Runaway'; The Monkees' 'Daydream Believer'; Elvis' 'Can't Help Falling in Love'; Frankie Valli's 'I Love You Baby' (a real classic which, sadly, we don't sing any more); Sham 69's 'Hersham Boys' (adapted to North Bank Boys); and The Clash's 'White Riot'.

Then there is the Kevin Johns' 'This is our day' battle-cry on the pitch at Wembley before the play-off final. His rabble-rousing call to arms contained the following magnificent lines: 'Reading have just sung a lovely song. From Glee. Which is lovely. But at Swansea we have our own song . . .' Cue absolute mayhem.

Check it out on YouTube. It's brilliant! Kevin is clearly a genius, and to my mind was he was Man of the Match on that great day.

West Swansea Plastics should note that Rev Kev was not talking about 'Hymns and Arias', but probably the greatest football song ever written, 'The Swansea City Song' penned by Roger Evans.

So, let's be 'avin' you, as Delia Smith once implored the crowd at Norwich. All together now:

'Swansea, Oh Swansea,
Oh City, said I;
I'll be standing on The North Bank,
Until the day I die;
Take me to the Vetch Field,
Way down by the sea;
Where I will follow Swansea, Swansea City!'

Come on, you Plastics at the back. Sing!

SATURDAY 23 FEBRUARY:

D-DAY -1

Finally, we're on our way. The Jack Army is on the march. From around the world to Wembley. Old and young; the long, the short, and the tall. A 36,000-strong motley crew is on the move, including the following 'Jackademics' and fellow travellers:

Huw Landeg Morris

Founder of YJB Tours Ltd. A frighteningly efficient man with an eye for detail and the main chance. 'Wembley tickets and travel. How may I help you?' Already has coaches booked (provisionally, it must be stressed) for next season's trips to all points east of Cadiz.

The Morris boys at Wembley: I know it was cold but I'm not sure about the head gear

John Conibear

His first Swans game was the Arsenal cup-tie in 1926. Yes, that's right, 1926, the year of the General Strike, the signing of the Locarno Treaty, and the setting up of Route 66 in the USA. So John's definitely not a Plastic then, and in fact this remarkable supporter is a walking encyclopaedia on the Swans. Somebody should write a book about him (winks).

'Mad' Peter Stead.

A tactical genius whose brutal assessment of games leads him to one of two conclusions: 'Awful' or 'Awesome'. Usually it's the former.

Elizabeth Stead

We are letting her come with us even though she openly boasts that the Swans are only her 'fourth favourite team'.

Martin Johnes: Wales' leading sports historian. Unfortunately his reputation is now in tatters because he came last (out of 90 entrants) in the great Jackademics Swans Quiz on the coaches to Wembley. He scored a pitiful 12 out of 20 and then claimed that he hadn't 'read the questions properly'

'Mad' Martin Johnes

Has forged a career out of intellectualising our collective love of watching twenty-two men kicking a bit of plastic about in a field. I'm never sure whether he would prefer to play for the Swans or be Fish from Marillion. I suspect that, deep down, it's the latter.

Huw Richards aka the Newshound

By some distance the best-ever writer about the Swans, especially when he out-Hornbyed Nick Hornby in a book edited by Nick Hornby. I still haven't forgiven him, though, for failing to save a key part of my Swans archive when an overheating of his mobile phone led to him burning down his flat in Walthamstow. Why on earth didn't you go back in, man?

A motley crew on Wembley Way: c'mon Huw Richards, mun. Cheer up, it's a blydi cup final!

Nick 'Chunky' Wroe

We think we saw our first Swans game together, but we can't remember when it was or who it was against. We think we were taken by 'the woman', but we don't know who she was. Always 'good in the air', Chunky is now without doubt the tallest literary critic in the world.

Peter White

A Turk masquerading as a Jack, he is going to get a smack round the back of the head if he emails me once more to ask, 'Have the tickets arrived yet?'

The Charles family

Members (allegedly) of Swansea's very own royal dynasty. Peter is the high-flying financial whizz-kid who famously provoked a heated exchange with Roary the Lion at Macclesfield. He is married to the only Cockney ever to be called Bethan. Just to prove to their neighbours in Northamptonshire that they really are Welsh, they named their children Carys and Gethin. Carys qualifies as the real fan, though, having been taken as a six month-old babe in arms to the most important game in the history of the Swans: Rochdale away in 2003.

Carys and Bethan Charles:
two babes at Wembley

Paul and Len Margetson. Len was always a jester, and here he proves it

Len Margetson

I haven't seen Len in a while but he warrants a mention here because I deeply admire his ability to hurl epithets and abuse at referees at the very top of his voice, often when he has said nothing at all for 20 minutes. My favourite volley of his was when he bellowed at Bramall Lane: 'Ref! You're about as useful as a Tesco trolley with a wobbly wheel!'

Raymond Ciborowski

Once a Mackem, now a Jackem. Crazy name, crazy guy (only joking, Mr Registrar).

Alun Burge

A recent free transfer into the club. Alun is a misty-eyed romantic from the Rhondda (or is it Blackwood?) who claims that the Swans are to Welsh soccer what Pontypridd RFC are to Welsh rugby. I'm sure he must be right because he usually is.

Geraint Jenkins

Known to all as Professor Pessimism, he taught me everything I don't know. He's not just in the glass half-empty camp, he's in the 'My glass is half-empty and I've also dropped it on the concrete floor' camp. He is confidently predicting that the Swans will not only lose to Bradford but also be relegated.

Ann Ffrancon

Glamorous wife of the above, who must possess the patience of a saint. She has our sympathy, but then lets herself down badly by revealing an unhealthy desire to be in a hospitality box.

Gwenno Ffrancon

Fortunately for her she has inherited the good looks and winsome smile of her mother and not the dark, brooding countenance of her father, which might suggest that . . . No, let's not go there.

Steve Thompson

Husband of the above. In my mind's eye I always see Steve playing the lead role in *Meet the Fockers*. I don't know why.

Siân Roberts

My delightful sister, who has very recently become a member of the West Swansea Plastics. Known in the family as 'Stan' because a letter she wrote to Father Christmas (when she was seventeen) was misread by one of Santa's little helpers, and the reply was framed accordingly. It's no wonder she's got issues.

Helen's gang: Amy, Spence, Mike, and Matthew

Dave Roberts

Long-suffering husband of the above. A Gog who has an uncanny ability to sniff out a good bottle of red, which is why he is so at home in the Platinum Lounge at the Liberty.

But, of course, I must also mention absent friends, particularly those who did the painful hard yards when we slogged our way around the lower leagues, with little hope and even less entertainment. I think especially of the late, great Richard Lillicrap who did so much to get the Supporters' Trust up and running, not just in Swansea but at other clubs.

A remarkable guy, Rich looked like a cross between Worzel Gummidge and the lead singer of Jethro Tull. He died far too young, but I know will be looking down on us tomorrow, a pint of real ale in one hand and a roll-up in the other, grinning his broken-toothed grin from ear to ear. And, like the rest of us, he'll give a loud and deafening answer when the question is put by Kevin Johns:

Who are we?

Jack Army!

Bowen and Morris at Wembley – the two Huws on Wembley Way. 'You're just a couple of rent boys' chanted some of the passing hordes as we attempted to pose for this picture

SUNDAY 24 FEBRUARY:

THE BIG DAY

Obviously there is no diary entry for today because I was busy doing other things, but the game was neatly summed up by Stan Collymore who (allegedly) shouted out during the 'live' radio commentary on TalkSport:

'Swansea are absolutely tearing Bradford to shrimps!'

I couldn't have put it better myself.

MONDAY 25 FEBRUARY:

WELCOME TO CLOUD NINE

Amazing! Wow! Simply the Best!

No, not really. But definitely the fourth best day of my life.

Enjoyable, fun, stress-free, and so, so, satisfying. I even managed to read some Proust on the bus, while my colleagues attempted (successfully by the sounds of it) to solve Fermat's Last Theorem. High fives.

So what have I learned from this remarkable, astonishing, dizzying experience?

- The only thing that anyone will ever remember about this series of articles (if they remember anything at all) is that I once owned a piece of inflatable fruit (cheers for that, Ceri Gould).
  (Note to obviously worried Vice-Chancellor. Ownership of inflatable fruit should not be taken seriously or to imply anything at all. It is simply a post-modern, ironic comment on the place of the football supporter in modern society. Plus, it's blydi good fun. You should try it. It is just a shame that my banana is now punctured beyond repair. Otherwise you could borrow it for Varsity.)
- Bradford City fans are the coolest, nicest people around. All of them. But especially the lovely lady who had travelled from Greece and who sat next to me. She is a tour operator who was so shell-shocked after number four went in that she forgot to give me her telephone number. I know, I'm sorry Huw Morris, and you can bet that we'll now definitely get Panathinaikos in the Europa League.
- When suitably galvanised by a coach leader's very public use of yellow and red cards, even academics can (eventually) come to understand that 'A 30-minute stop at Reading services' does actually mean 'A 30-minute stop at Reading services'. I'm sorry, but what on earth were you thinking of, cheerfully tucking in to a Full Monty and doing the crossword while the rest of us were on the buses waiting for you? Yes, you know who you are. And no, you can't come again.
- Les the coach driver did actually know what he was doing, despite the faulty sat nav. And despite the fact that we appeared to be

The Great Dane

speeding away from Wembley less than two hours before kick-off. How many times did I have to say, 'I'm sorry. Les is the driver, and you are only Professor Emeritus in Welsh History. Now please sit down'?

- Despite what I might just have hinted at in a previous entry, 'Hymns and Arias' is actually not bad. Sorry, Max. But couldn't you just have speeded it up a bit?

- To enjoy fully the winning Wembley experience, you do have to be in the cheapest seats right behind the goal, as I was. I just don't understand why on earth anyone would want to be schmoozing in a nice, warm corporate hospitality box.

So, the dust finally begins to settle on a riotous, rollicking, rampant weekend for the Swans.

By the way and while I remember: does anyone know how Wales got on in the rugby? I couldn't find anything about it in *Wales on Sunday*.

And how do I feel about it all?

Well, it's simple really. I am so, so proud today. Bursting, like.

I am SOOOO proud of my team, my club, my city, my university, my newspaper, my friends, my family (especially my sister Stan x), my colleagues (well, some of them), and even the West Swansea Plastics (just for today, mind).

The Jackademics flag is flown proudly at the Victory parade. Only Cybil the Swan takes any notice

I am SOOOO proud of Michael Laudrup (please stay for ever, you know it makes sense), Huw Jenkins, Don and Gaynor Keefe, Martin Morgan, Kevin Johns, Steve and Anne Penny, Dorian Heel Bar, my all-time hero Curt, Little Leon, Monkey, Tatey, Car Boot Ashley, Ben Davies, the Spanish Armada led by the Admirable Admiral Angel, and all of the rest of the United Nations down the Liberty. And anyone else I have forgotten.

Boys (and girls), you all done us proud! I luvs you all! You are all proper tidy, like. Every one of you. Cowing lush!

Who are we again?

JACK ARMY!

POSTSCRIPT

I am now lying down in a darkened room for a while. Then YJB Travel, Tours, and Exports Ltd will start to take bookings for the Europa League third-round away leg to be played in Azerbaijan. Or, more likely, knowing our luck, in Inverness.

THE CAPITAL ONE CUP FINAL MATCH REPORT

Courtesy of the *Western Mail*

Swansea City v Bradford City match report

Due to the sheer joy of this day, you will have noticed that I couldn't write a single word to describe the match itself. Luckily, the *Western Mail* did it justice, so here is the match report.

Swansea City 5 - 0 Bradford City: Majestic Swans win Capital Cup

SWANSEA CITY secured a historic first major trophy with a thumping victory over Bradford City in the Capital One Cup final.

The Wembley final proved a step too far for the League Two side who were well-beaten by Michael Laudrup's stylish Swans.

A double from Nathan Dyer, Michu's 19th goal of the season and two from Jonathan de Guzman gave Swansea their maiden major cup win in their centenary season.

Bradford goalkeeper Matt Duke was sent off in the second half as Phil Parkinson's side put on a brave display against a Swansea side ranked 70 league places above them.

Swansea's win beat the record League Cup final winning margin set by Manchester United with their 4-0 win over Wigan in 2006.

Victory means Laudrup's side will play in the Europa League third qualifying round next season, the first time Swansea have qualified for Europe since 1991.

Bradford had knocked three top flight sides out of the competition on their way to Wembley but there was to be no fairytale finish to the Bantams incredible story.

Instead it was Swansea, playing in League Two just 10 years ago, who capped their own remarkable rags to riches rise with a Welsh club's first major trophy since 1927.

They have enjoyed a brilliant season under former Real Madrid and Barcelona legend Laudrup and the gulf in quality between the two sides was evident from the first whistle as Swansea took full control of the contest.

Only some indecision in the final third stopped Swansea testing Duke in the opening quarter of an hour but it wasn't long before Laudrup's side were making their mark in the game.

Good build up work from Swansea saw Angel Rangel find left back Ben Davies at the back post but the Neath-born youngster's header bounced narrowly wide.

A minute later Swansea were in front from a lovely flowing move that had begun as a Bradford counter-attack.

Garry Thompson's cross was cleared to de Guzman in the centre of midfield and he quickly set the Swans on their way.

De Guzman and Wayne Routledge combined to find Michu on the edge of the box and when his shot was saved by Duke it was Dyer who reacted quickest to tap the ball in at the back post.

It was everything Swansea deserved for a confident opening and Parkinson's side just couldn't get the ball off their Premier League opponents.

Long-serving midfielder Leon Britton went close with a long-range effort on the half hour mark and it looked like only a matter of time before Swansea would double their advantage.

Their second came five minutes before the break when another sweeping counter-attack ended with Pablo Hernandez finding Michu in the box,

he was given too much time to turn and placed a neat finish into the bottom corner.

Hernandez and Routledge then forced saves out of Duke in quick succession before the break and Swansea sensed a chance to finish the contest early.

That's exactly what happened two minutes into the second half when Dyer broke down the right, exchanged passes with Routledge before cutting back inside onto his left foot and firing into the top corner.

After that it was damage limitation for Bradford but their afternoon went from bad to worse when Duke was sent off for a foul on de Guzman.

Michu played a ball into de Guzman in the box and when he got their ahead of Duke the keeper caught the Dutchman and referee Kevin Friend was left with little option.

De Guzman eventually stepped up to take the penalty after a long argument with Dyer, who felt he should be allowed to complete his hat-trick, and placed a smart finish past substitute goalkeeper Jon McLaughlin.

Swans boss Laudrup sent club captain Garry Monk on in place of Ki Sung Yueng shortly after the fourth goal and it was a nice touch by the Dane for a player who had captained the Swans in all four divisions in his eight years with the club.

The final 15 minutes were nothing more than a victory parade for Laudrup's side in front of 36,000 ecstatic Swansea supporters.

McLaughlin looked to have denied Swansea a fifth when he saved brilliantly from Michu in the final moments before Dwight Tiendalli hit the crossbar for the Swans.

But de Guzman completed the rout with a close range finish from Rangel's cross from the right in injury time.

BRADFORD v SWANSEA KEY MOMENTS

14 minutes: Angel Rangel clips over an inviting cross to the far post and Swansea left-back Ben Davies powers a downward header inches wide of Bradford goalkeeper Matt Duke's left-hand post.

16: GOAL. Swansea midfielder Wayne Routledge collects the ball in his own half and is allowed to run unopposed deep into Bradford territory before finding Michu on the left edge of the penalty area. The Spaniard's low shot is parried by Bradford goalkeeper Matt Duke, but Nathan Dyer follows up to force home the rebound.

31: Jonathan De Guzman's corner is headed clear by Bradford defender Rory McArdle, but only as far as Leon Britton lurking just outside the penalty area and the diminutive Swansea midfielder crashes a right-footed volley wide.

35: In Bradford's penalty area McArdle stretches out a leg just in time to divert the ball away from Swansea striker Michu, who would otherwise have had a clear path to goal.

40: GOAL. Pablo Hernandez nutmegs Bradford skipper Gary Jones with a pass to find Michu on the left edge of the area and the Swansea forward has plenty of time to pick his spot before curling a low left-footed shot through the legs of Bradford defender Carl McHugh and inside the far post to make it 2-0.

47: GOAL. Michu steps over Routledge's pass into the penalty area to allow the ball to run on to Dyer and the winger cuts inside Bradford's substitute defender Andrew Davies before curling a fine shot high inside Duke's right-hand post to make it 3-0 and kill the game.

56: RED CARD. Jonathan De Guzman is sent clear on goal following Dyer's deft pass but is brought crashing down by goalkeeper Matt Duke's outstretched leg, leaving referee Kevin Friend with no choice other than to show the Bradford number one a straight red card.

59: GOAL. After substitute goalkeeper Jon McLaughlin had been sent on for striker Nahki Wells, De Guzman, who won an argument with two-goal Dyer over who should take the spot-kick, plants the ball into the bottom left corner to put the result beyond doubt.

87: Swansea substitute Dwight Tiendalli curls a right-footed shot beyond the stranded McLaughlin and against the post as Michael Laudrup's side chase a fifth goal.

90: GOAL. Swansea right-back Angel Rangel charges forward once more and crosses into the area with pace for De Guzman to clip home his second goal and Swansea's fifth.

THEY THOUGHT IT WAS ALL OVER . . .

Shortly before this book went to print, Cardiff City gained promotion to the Premier League, joining Swansea City and making the league ten per cent Welsh. This was my reaction in the *Western Mail* the following day.

Cardiff go up: a view from Swansea

Okay. Here we go. Pause. Deep breath. Well done Cardiff City. Congratulations on your promotion to the Premier League.

There, I've said it. And, actually, I do mean it, even though those words will cost me several friendships and lead to heckling on the streets of Swansea.

I am pleased for Cardiff and their proverbially 'long-suffering' fans. I am very pleased for Welsh football. And I am very, very pleased for Wales and its struggling economy.

For Wales to have two sides in the Premier League is genuinely astonishing, not least because not too long ago, both Cardiff and Swansea were basket-case clubs run by chancers who turned them into laughing stocks.

For the benefit of younger readers who might doubt this, let us turn the clock back sixteen years. Yes, just sixteen years.

On 3 December 1996 the Swans beat Cardiff 3-1 at Ninian Park in front of a crowd of 3,721 people. Okay, there were off-the-field reasons to explain in part this pathetically small attendance. And of course tiny crowds were also a feature of derby games played at the Vetch.

But the main reason that fans had turned their backs on the two clubs was that the footballing fare on offer was, as Peter Stead would say, awful with a capital A. This meant that to admit back then that you were a Swan or a Bluebird was to invite ridicule and pity.

Things got so bad that at the end of the 1997-98 season the Swans finished 88th of the 92 clubs in the Football League. To some small-minded fans this was regarded as a triumph because Cardiff trailed in one place behind in 89th position! But let's be honest, what is the point of claiming local 'bragging rights' if that prize has to be won in the bargain basement, the dungeon of 'English' football?

Of course, I realise that I am in a small minority when I offer congratulations to Cardiff. Already the message boards are awash with exchanges of banter.

Two years ago, when the Swans were promoted, Cardiff fans gleefully predicted that Wales's first Premier League team would 'do a Derby' and return straight back to the Championship. Now Swans fans are suggesting the same, with some welcoming Cardiff's elevation because this will serve up an easy six points next season.

Then there are the tedious 'we're bigger than you' boasts, along with the 'we are your capital' stuff. To which the answer is 'We are your Capital One Cup holders'. And so on.

Most of these exchanges are harmless and good-natured attempts at a wind-up.

But, no doubt, Neanderthals and knuckle-scrapers in both camps are already planning their punch-ups and acts of violence of the type seen in Newcastle city centre last weekend. It is for this reason that some are suggesting that South Wales Police are already planning to cancel all leave as soon as the dates of the two derby games are announced.

In fact, the people with the most to worry about are probably those in charge of the WRU and the regional rugby sides. Having taken the astonishing decision to confine professional rugby in Wales to four 'regions' which do not play in the game's traditional Valley heartlands, the administrators and bean-counters are now faced with the prospect of every young child and floating sports fan in Wales being captivated by the self-styled 'greatest show on earth' that is football's Premier League.

There is no doubt about it – the hottest tickets in Wales next season will be at the Liberty and Cardiff City Stadium (or whatever they will be called), and the WRU had better hope that the Welsh team continues to do well. Because if it doesn't, Welsh rugby will have an even bumpier ride than it is already experiencing.

But, hey, let's not worry too much about fate of our so-called 'national game'. What about the Swans and Cardiff next season?

As far as the Swans are concerned, will it be possible to combine a demanding Europa League with the battle to get to the magic 40 points? Certainly, the club continues to astonish and amaze as it takes giant strides forward each year. Indeed, we now have so much faith in Chairman Huw and his board that the fans seem much more relaxed about losing key personnel on and off the pitch each summer. Having said that, don't go Ashley!

There does indeed seem to be a blueprint for success at Swansea. I wouldn't for one moment suggest that Cardiff might like to adopt the 'Swansea Way'. But it is worth reflecting on why the Swans have been able to establish themselves in the top half of the table and, as a bonus, win some proper silverware for the first time.

My own non-expert view is that to make a successful (and gigantic) step up from the Championship, clubs must already have in their team five or six players who are capable of playing at a higher level. This core group provides two key things: continuity and identity.

The Swans were fortunate to have an abundance of such players: Angel Rangel, Neil Taylor, Ashley Williams, Garry Monk, Leon Britton, Nathan Dyer, Joe Allen, and Scott Sinclair. All of these players have improved and grown to become established Premier League players, so much so that some of them are no longer with the Swans!

It is to this core that have been added the more exotic talents such as Michu and Chico. Twenty years ago, did I ever think I would watch a Swans team containing names such as these? No, of course not.

Have Cardiff got such a core of players? I don't know, because I never watch them play. But one thing is for sure. Attempting to build a team from scratch to compete in the Premier League often provides a one-way ticket to oblivion. Witness the slow-motion car-crash that is Queen's Park Rangers.

So, good luck to the Bluebirds, Redbirds, or whatever you are today. Welcome to the Big Time!